Living Single

TONY EVANS

MOODY PUBLISHERS
CHICAGO

All Scripture quotations, unless otherwise indicated, are taken from the *New
American Standard Bible*®, Copyright © 1960, 1962, 1963, 1968, 1971, 1972, 1973,
1975, 1977, 1995 by The Lockman Foundation. Used by permission. (www.Lock-
man.org)

Scripture quotations marked NIV are taken from the Holy Bible, New International Version®, NIV® Copyright © 1973, 1978, 1984, 2011 by Biblica,
Inc.™ Used by permission of Zondervan. All rights reserved worldwide.
www.zondervan.com. The "NIV" and "New International Version" are trademarks
registered in the United States Patent and Trademark Office by Biblica, Inc.™

Edited by Jim Vincent
Interior design: Ragont Design
Cover design: Thinkpen Design
Cover image:© 2013 Shutterstock image #51503998

Library of Congress Cataloging-in-Publication Data

Evans, Tony, 1949-
 Living single / Tony Evans.
    pages cm
 ISBN 978-0-8024-1010-8
 1. Single people--Religious life. I. Title.
 BV4596.S5E928 2013
 248..8'4--dc23

                        2013016458

Moody Publishers is committed to caring wisely for God's creation
and uses recycled paper whenever possible. The paper in this book
consists of 10 percent post-consumer waste.

We hope you enjoy this book from Moody Publishers. Our goal is to provide high-
quality, thought-provoking books and products that connect truth to your real needs
and challenges. For more information on other books and products written and produced from a biblical perspective, go to www.moodypublishers.com or write to:

Moody Publishers
820 N. LaSalle Boulevard
Chicago, IL 60610

1 3 5 7 9 10 8 6 4 2

Printed in the United States of America

CONTENTS

Introduction	5
1. Waiting on the Lord	11
2. Working for the Lord	35
3. Wedded in the Lord	57
The Urban Alternative	81

INTRODUCTION

A pastor who happens to be married is always on dangerous ground when he approaches the issue of singleness. Invariably he hears the accusation, "Pastor, you don't understand. You've been married for so long. By the time you knew what singleness meant, you weren't single anymore!"

It's natural for people to feel that you cannot relate to them because you haven't experienced what they are experiencing. However, the truth of the Word transcends our experiences. I have never been an alcoholic, but I can tell you what the Bible has to say about it. I can speak because God has spoken.

Nevertheless, I understand the need of many of you to hear from someone who knows firsthand what the single

lifestyle is really like. That's why I have chosen to borrow
heavily for the content of this booklet from the words of
someone who was single for a very long time, even
though he probably was married at some point in his life.

I'm talking about the apostle Paul.

The apostle Paul understood the single lifestyle far
better than the social commentators of our day. His inspired words in the New Testament present us with a
challenge that cuts across the grain of our society:

Being single is more desirable for a Christian than being married.

There's a good deal of controversy surrounding that
concept, even though it is every bit as biblical as John
3:16. Make no mistake about what Paul is saying: *If you are
single, you are in the best possible position.*

A single woman was talking with her pastor one day,
discussing the subject of marriage. The pastor said, "You
know, God has designed the perfect plan for marriage:
one man and one woman together for life. You can't improve on God's plan."

"Pastor, I don't want to improve on it," the woman
replied. "I just want to get in on it."

That's the way many single people feel today. They
fear they are missing out on God's plan or God's best for
their lives because they aren't married. Many singles feel
as if their lives are in a holding pattern, like an airplane
that is supposed to be landing at its destination but has
been ordered to circle the airport.

I've flown enough to know what it's like for the pilot
to come on the intercom and announce that the plane has

been denied permission to land for whatever reason. Holding patterns are very frustrating because you are helpless. You didn't choose the situation, and there is nothing you can do about it. All you know is that you want the pilot to get the plane on the ground so you can get off of it.

One particular time when this happened to me, it seemed like we had been circling for hours. I kept looking at my watch and then looking out the window to see if there was any indication that we were moving closer to the earth. After enough times of going back and forth between my wrist and the window, I decided that I would take out some work that I had brought with me and focus on it instead. Before long, I became so involved with what I was doing that I forgot we were still in a holding pattern altogether.

Singles, God has so much for you to do while you are waiting for a mate, and He can satisfy you so fully with what you are doing that you literally forget what you feel like you are missing out on.

I couldn't control how long the pilot kept us in the holding pattern in the sky. But I could control what I did with the time that I was up there. Likewise, I do not know how long it will be before God addresses your single-hood. What I do know is that He does not expect you to be wasting your time while waiting. He wants you to wait on Him for direction, sure, but to do so in the context of maximizing living single.

If you are a Christian single person who loves God

and wants to honor and serve Him with your life, then I want to speak to you from God's Word, because the Bible contains some very important, challenging, and encouraging principles for Christian singles. (These principles also have implications for married people, as we'll see.)

The Scripture deals with the subject of singleness head-on in 1 Corinthians 7:25–40, where the apostle Paul was in the process of answering his readers' questions concerning marriage and singleness. Paul was the right person to handle these issues, as I mentioned earlier, because the evidence suggests that he had been married at one time and then lived for many years as a single person. So he knew what it was like to have a mate and to be alone.

Paul must have been married because before his conversion he was a member of the Sanhedrin, the supreme council of Jewish leaders, which required its members to be married. Perhaps his wife had died, or she may even have left him when he came to Christ. The point is that Paul knew what it was like both to have a mate and to live as a single person.

There's another reason 1 Corinthians 7 is so important to the issue of marital status, which is that Paul was speaking by divine revelation. So what he wrote in this portion of Scripture is the Word of God and not just one man's opinion. And in 1 Corinthians 7 we find at least three vital principles for singles. We can summarize these as waiting on the Lord, working for the Lord, and being wedded in the Lord. These main components that make up much of what it means to be single will be the focus of our time together in this booklet, and it is my prayer that after reading it, you will not only embrace singlehood—if that is where God has you—but you will also maximize every moment in which you are single.

And while I want to acknowledge before we go deeper into singlehood that most people are probably not called to be single but they are single by default simply due to the sinful world in which we live (growing up in broken homes, not enough Kingdom-minded mates available to marry), Paul makes it clear that if you are single, God can make your situation a blessing rather than bitter if you look to Him to do it. If this is you, take courage and pride in your position because God Himself is your purpose. You have been made for Him. As He says in Isaiah, "'For your husband is your Maker, whose name is the Lord of hosts; and your Redeemer is the Holy One of Israel, Who is called the God of all the earth. For the Lord has called you, like a wife forsaken and grieved in spirit, even like a wife of one's youth when she is rejected,' says your God" (Isaiah 54:5, 6).

WAITING ON THE LORD

A lot of singles would look at this chapter title and say, "Oh, yeah, I know all about waiting. I've been waiting on the Lord to give me a mate for a long time."

Most singles would agree that they're waiting for an opportunity to marry, because they don't plan on being single the rest of their lives. God's concern for you as a waiting single is *how you are doing* while you're waiting. Let me show you what I mean by giving you a kingdom view of singlehood.

I am sure that many of you who picked up this booklet are frustrated singles. You are frustrated because you have been alone for a very long time without any prospect of marriage. There are others who are frustrated because you have been in and out of one unhealthy relationship after another simply because you are willing to lower your standards in order to avoid the feeling of being alone. Paul knows something of singlehood, so his words on this matter can shed light on what many people today are going through.

Paul had been discussing marriage and divorce in 1 Corinthians 7:1–24 before turning to the specific issue of singleness in verse 25: "Now concerning virgins I have no command of the Lord, but I give an opinion as one who by the mercy of the Lord is trustworthy."

When Paul said the Lord had not given a command about being single, he meant that when Jesus was on earth He didn't speak directly to this issue. Jesus certainly could have spoken on singleness, because He experienced the single life to the *n*th degree, including the temptations that singles face.

But God chose instead to entrust His message on singleness and its principles to Paul. My point is that when Paul said he was offering his view, he was saying, "I have the Lord's mind on this." This is important because some people try to discount Paul's teaching here as of lesser authority than Jesus' words. But the Bible knows no such distinction.

WAIT IN MORAL PURITY

Notice that when Paul began to discuss unmarried people, he used the term *virgins* in 1 Corinthians 7:25. For Paul, singleness was synonymous with virginity, and so the first principle in waiting is to maintain your moral purity.

In the divine context, if you are single and you love the Lord, you are also celibate. The two go hand in hand. Paul was referring primarily to physical virginity or sexual purity, although there is also a spiritual purity that people who have been sexually immoral can recapture. We'll talk about that too.

God not only anticipates and expects, but also demands, that single people be celibate. Now this is a difficult message in a day of license, liberty, and hedonism. We've gone from the Victorian Age to Victoria's Secret catalogs. Victoria even has her own racy television ads. Modesty has been thrown to the wind. Yet we are not called to adapt the Bible to our age, but to adapt our age to the Bible.

Sex today has been cheapened by a world that does not have a divine perspective. And things that are cheap can be given away easily. Things that are valuable, you protect.

My single friend, your sense of value will be measured in large part by your morality. Many people treat sex like the all-night drive-through at the local fast-food restaurant—always available when the desire hits you. Purity is no longer a priority.

But the Bible says equally to men and to women that God's desire and design for singles is their moral purity. Sex in God's hand is holy. Sex in the devil's hand is death. One of the major ways that Satan promotes his program in history is through illicit sex. For example, Satan used

> # MANY PEOPLE TREAT SEX LIKE THE ALL-NIGHT FAST-FOOD DRIVE-THROUGH—ALWAYS AVAILABLE WHEN THE DESIRE HITS YOU.

sexual relations between unholy men and the "daughters of men" to produce an ungodly race in an attempt to destroy God's plan for the world (see Genesis 6:1–2).

Since God commands purity for singles, how can a single person embrace this demand when our natural desires and our sexuality are so much a part of our DNA? To answer that, let me show you a crucial principle in Paul's thinking that comes out of this same letter to the Corinthians. The principle is that as Christians we are not to view sex as purely a biological matter, but as a spiritual one.

In 1 Corinthians 6:13 Paul wrote, "Food is for the stomach and the stomach is for food, but God will do away with both of them. Yet the body is not for immorality, but for the Lord, and the Lord is for the body."

Notice the contrast between the way we treat hunger, a legitimate physical appetite, and the way we should treat our bodies when it comes to sexual morality. Most people in Corinth, a very wicked city, equated food with sex. When they got hungry, they ate. When they wanted sex, they fed that appetite. Corinth even had a temple with a restaurant on one side and a brothel on the other. A person could have dinner at the restaurant and go to the brothel for dessert. No big deal.

No, Paul says, it's a very big deal. It's okay to eat when you're hungry because the stomach was made for food. But it's not okay to indulge in sex whenever you feel like it because your body was not made for sexual immorality. This is where Paul begins to make the switch from the purely physical to the spiritual view of sex—which he will expand on in verses 15–20.

But notice verse 14, which explains how singles can remain sexually pure when everything around them says to go ahead and indulge their appetites. "Now God has not only raised the Lord, but will also raise us up through His power."

This might seem out of place at first. What does Christ's resurrection and our future resurrection have to do with a Christian's sexual purity? Everything, because Paul is saying that we have the same power working within us that raised Jesus from the dead. If God can raise Jesus from the dead, He can give us the power to remain pure even in a decadent culture.

How Spiritual Is It?

How spiritual is this matter of sex for a Christian? Paul answers that by beginning with a question: "Do you not know that your bodies are members of Christ? Shall I then take away the members of Christ and make them members of a prostitute? May it never be!" (1 Corinthians 6:15).

Why was Paul so adamant about this? Because the truth of our spiritual union with Christ means that whatever we do, we bring Jesus into it with us. In other words, whenever you as a Christian are sexually intimate with another person, you are making Jesus participate with you.

God has given His blessing to sex within the marriage union, but if the sexual activity is outside of marriage it's the equivalent of spiritual rape. Paul was horrified at the thought, and we should be too.

Why is sex so devastating both physically and spiritually when it is misused? We find the answer to that in 1 Corinthians 6:16–18. "Or do you not know that the one who joins himself to a prostitute is one body with her? For He says, 'The two shall become one flesh'" (v. 16). Paul says that a unique spiritual union is created by the sex act, even when it is done as an act of immorality between two people who have no intention of forming a lasting relationship.

We know this because Paul used God's own words from the first marriage (see Genesis 2:24) to describe a temporary sexual union. Even if a man would probably never consider walking down the aisle with a woman he used for a "one-night stand," there is a sense in which he *did* walk down the aisle with her.

To be sure, their union was a false one, but the fact is their sexual union formed a one-flesh relationship that also included a fusion of their souls. It's as if these two people each stamped a part of his or her soul on the other person. Therefore, when they separate, each leaves behind a part of him or herself with the other person, creating tremendous spiritual damage.

That's why the idea of illicit or casual sex as a one-time encounter that's over and done the next morning is the furthest thing from the truth. Many people who have been sexually immoral can testify to painful memories that play themselves back because God designed sex as a spiritual and not merely a biological reality.

> GOD HAS DESIGNED SEX AS
> A SPIRITUAL AND NOT MERELY
> A BIOLOGICAL REALITY.

Instead of two people joining themselves together sexually outside of marriage, God has a higher standard: "But the one who joins himself to the Lord is one spirit with Him" (v. 17). There must be a spiritual oneness with the Lord that overrides the desire for illegitimate physical oneness with another person.

And so God's advice to singles or anyone tempted to engage in illicit activity is "Flee immorality." Do you remember the story of Joseph? When he was young, his jealous brothers sold him into slavery. He wound up in Egypt where he was purchased by Potiphar, the captain of Pharaoh's personal guard. Joseph was a faithful servant, and as God watched over him and blessed his work, his master prospered. Eventually, Joseph became Potiphar's "main man"—the overseer of the house and custodian of everything Potiphar owned.

It was at this point that he captured the attention of Potiphar's wife. She didn't give a thought to Joseph when he was brought into the house as a ragged, dirty slave. But now he was clean, well built, and handsome. So, with the class and charm typical of an Egyptian royal woman in that day, she walked up to Joseph and said, "Come to bed with me." Of course, Joseph refused. But he offered a pointed explanation: "My master does not concern himself with anything in the house, and he has put all he owns in my charge. There is no one greater in this house than I, and he has withheld nothing from me except you, because you are his wife. How then could I do this great evil and sin against God?" (Genesis 39:8–9).

Joseph's resistance became an obstacle that Potiphar's wife was determined to overcome. She spoke to Joseph day after day, but couldn't wear down his resolve. It was time to engineer a more aggressive plan.

One day, Joseph entered the house to find it empty. Hardly by coincidence were the household servants gone.

Potiphar's wife grabbed Joseph by his cloak and said, "Come to bed with me!" But the Bible tells us that Joseph left the cloak in her hand and ran out of the house.

"Flee immorality," Paul writes in 1 Corinthians 6:18. That's what Joseph did. And that's what we must do, too.

Why? "All other sins a person commits are outside the body, but whoever sins sexually, sins against their own body" (6:18). Translation: *sexual sin is self-destructive.* It's like a fire. A fire in the fireplace can do you a lot of good. A fire in the living room will mess up your whole house! And that's precisely the case with our sexuality. It is a fire to be kindled only within the fireplace of marriage. Outside of that safe enclosure, it can do all kinds of emotional and physical damage.

> OUR SEXUALITY IS A FIRE TO BE KINDLED ONLY WITHIN THE FIREPLACE OF MARRIAGE. OTHERWISE IT CAN DO ALL KINDS OF DAMAGE.

Then Paul asked another important question. "Or do you not know that your body is a temple of the Holy Spirit who is in you, whom you have from God, and that you are not your own? For you have been bought with a price: therefore glorify God in your body" (vv. 19–20).

We can see the spiritual nature of sex here because Paul referred to our bodies as temples with which we can glorify God. A temple is a church house, the place where God is worshiped. This means that when a husband and wife engage in sex, they are actually participating in an act of worship. Single, if you have any doubt about whether your behavior—sexual or otherwise—is appropriate, just remember that you take Jesus with you wherever you go. Will you be able to look at Jesus wherever you go? He is right there with you. Will you be able to look at Him after doing whatever you are contemplating and say, "Jesus, did you enjoy yourself?" If not, leave your coat and run for the door.

If you are in Christ, you are now the personal property of the King of kings and Lord of lords. On the receipt, the price is clearly marked: "Paid in full by the blood of the Lamb." The church today needs a group of holy singles who will honor God with their bodies. We need young ladies who can say "no." We need to teach our daughters to say, "I'm saving myself for that man God has chosen for me, whenever he comes into my life."

Please do not misunderstand me. I am not saying that sexual desire is inappropriate. You should not be praying that God would remove your sexual drive. Instead, pray that He will enable you to control that energy until the time is right to unleash it. There are good reasons— theological, ethical, and medical—for remaining sexually pure. But the truth is, it isn't easy. The world places a high value on conformity, and those who don't measure up to the image of the "liberated single" experience pressure.

Virginity is held in disregard today, much the same as promiscuity once was. Ridicule and perhaps even pressure to conform can be expected. In fact, even Joseph, who remained so faithful, was accused of rape by Potiphar's wife. He would spend thirteen years in prison because of that false accusation.

Beyond possible ridicule and feeling the pressure to conform, our own bodies may even fight against us. After all, our sex drive doesn't shut down just because we decide to keep ourselves pure.

Yet Paul reminds us that our bodies are now the temple of the most High God. As singles, we are to treat our bodies with the honor they deserve. This is an awesome illustration of the spiritual nature of our sexuality. In the Old Testament, a person who wanted to get close to God went into the temple to worship. And in the deepest recess of the temple was a place called the Holy of Holies, the most sacred part of the temple hidden behind a veil. No one could enter there but the high priest, and then only once a year with blood to cover the people's sins.

God has created every woman with a bodily veil called a hymen. This creates a covering that literally says what the Old Testament said about the Holy of Holies— no trespassing until such time as it is appropriate to shed blood.

That's why it is common for a woman who is a virgin

to shed blood on her wedding night. There is a breaking of the veil, the hymen, by the only person rightfully allowed to do that, the woman's husband-priest. Sexual intercourse between a husband and wife is a holy act.

OUR BODIES RESTORED TO PURITY

What about single men and women who will not be able to know this wedding-night experience in the way God intended because they have already had sex outside of marriage? Let's be clear that illicit sex is sin, but the Bible also has a word of hope and restoration for singles who have failed morally.

Judging from Paul's message in 1 Corinthians, he was writing to a lot of people who had been immoral. No matter what they had done, Paul wrote, "But you were washed, but you were sanctified, but you were justified in the name of the Lord Jesus Christ" (1 Corinthians 6:11).

God can and will forgive sexual sin and restore any believer to purity. Those who have lost their physical virginity can still regain their spiritual virginity and purity of life before God. Spiritual virginity is when God gives you back what the devil took away.

You see, when God saved you He made you a diamond. If I rub a diamond in the dirt, what I have is a dirty diamond that has lost none of its intrinsic value. It just needs to be cleansed and restored to its original luster.

We can't change the past, but we can clean up the present and look forward to a shiny future. If you have compromised your moral purity and have not dealt with it before God, go to Him in confession and repentance and experience His cleansing (read 1 John 1:9 and claim its promise). If you are still a virgin and committed to sexual purity, ask God to help you stand strong. And remember, He has promised not to let you get in any situation without a way of escape (see 1 Corinthians 10:13).

WAIT WITH THE RIGHT MENTALITY

While you're waiting on the Lord, make sure that your thinking is straight too. Paul addressed this issue in verses 26–28 of 1 Corinthians 7.

Too many singles have only one thought on their minds: *I need to get married, no matter what.* But the Bible has a different emphasis. "I think then that this is good in view of the present distress, that it is good for a man to remain as he is" (v. 26). In other words, whether you're married or single, don't let your marital status dominate your thinking and focus.

Paul said this because he knew there were bigger things at stake in the Christian life than a person's marital status. This wouldn't be such a big deal for singles today except that we are guilty as a society and as a church of making single people feel like second-class citizens.

But God doesn't make any distinction between married and single people in terms of their value in His eyes. That's clear from what Paul said in 1 Corinthians 7:27:

"Are you bound to a wife? Do not seek to be released. Are you released from a wife? Do not seek a wife."

If singleness were not as acceptable to God as marriage, He would have commanded all Christians to get married, and Paul would probably have gotten married, or perhaps remarried, himself. The point is that singles are not worse off than married people.

In fact, marriage has its own set of challenges and problems. "If a virgin marries, she has not sinned. Yet such will have trouble in this life, and I am trying to spare you," Paul wrote in 1 Corinthians 7:28.

ARE YOU BETTER OFF SINGLE . . . OR MARRIED?

Now I know that many single Christians, especially older singles, become defensive when they hear this because they think, *Oh yes, here it comes, the old "You're better off single" speech that's supposed to make me feel better about not having anyone.*

That may be some people's reaction, but there's no denying the truth that from the standpoint of kingdom service, which was Paul's focus, singles are less encumbered than married people.

We also can't deny the truth that marriage is not an automatic fix for all the needs of single people. You may say, "But Tony, I'm lonely. I have to eat alone at night and go to bed alone. I have normal emotional longings and sexual needs that are not being fulfilled, and I'm frustrated."

Well, I've counseled many married people who are so emotionally lonely and/or sexually unsatisfied that they're thinking about bailing out on their marriages and going back to being single. *The only thing more painful than being single and miserable is being married and miserable.*

Let's get our thinking straight. Anyone who thinks marriage is the end-all and be-all of life, the answer to all of a single person's dreams and problems, is in for a big letdown. Marriage is wonderful, sometimes. Someone likened it once to flies on a window screen. Some are on the outside wanting in, and others are on the inside wanting out.

There's not an honest married person who will not tell you that marriage involves adjustments and problems along with the benefits. The question is not whether marriage or singleness is better, but what God's will is for each of His children in light of eternity's values.

When Paul says that he is trying to spare singles from the troubles they will find in marriage, he acknowledges the reality that what many people think they are getting on the front end isn't what they wind up with every day. Without a doubt, there are troubles in relationships.

One of the troubles and challenges in marriages is that you can no longer come and go as you please. If you are single, you can choose what you do with the freedom you experience with your time. But when you are married, you have to call and check in, let people know when you are getting home, and then even when you do get home—there is often a "honey-do" list for you to do now that you are home. Many married people often wind up feeling "hen-pecked" because they are bound not only by location and time, but by what they do when they spend their time at that location as well. To top it off, many married people aren't having nearly as much sexual intimacy as they once thought that they would, so the bondage of marriage comes with little perceived benefit. Singles are free from the concern and troubles that are often found in marriage.

When Paul said, "Do not seek a wife," he wasn't saying it's wrong to desire to be married. Instead, his focus was on methodology. The idea is, "Stop man-hunting or woman-hunting. Don't spend all your time searching for the right one."

Everywhere singles turn today they find someone trying to fix them up with a prospect, whether it's over the Internet, at church, or in the family. Single people used to play *The Dating Game* on television. But some people play it in real life. As a result, singles end up trying to grab someone or Google someone or find someone at the club. Paul is saying that he doesn't want you to go around with the attitude, "Let me find a mate—I need to find a mate . . . I've *got* to find a mate!" He knows that if you go out there and "find a mate," you are also going to find some trouble. Due to that reality, you want to be very careful in the process of linking up with somebody.

Let me ask you a question by first making a statement. Statistics tell us that roughly 50 percent of all marriages end in divorce in America. A large part of the other 50

> # SOME SINGLES END UP TRYING TO GRAB SOMEONE OR GOOGLE SOMEONE. . . "I'VE *GOT* TO FIND A MATE!"

percent stay together for convenience, finances, or the children. Here is my question: If 50 percent of all airplanes crashed, wouldn't you be extra careful about flying? If you knew that one out of every two airplanes was going to go down in flames, don't you think that you would do a real careful investigation before getting on a plane, simply because you wouldn't want to be one of those casualties?

The same answer should hold true for how you approach the potential of marriage. You need to be very careful before you link up with someone so that you don't end up as another statistic.

You don't have to cheapen yourself by playing the dating game. Adam found his wife when he was asleep. God put the boy out and crafted a wife for him and then brought Eve to Adam. I say that humorously but also seriously. God knows where you live. You don't have to spend all your time worrying about tracking down a mate or trying to be in all the right places to meet people. Get on with your life and service for God. He knows where to find you when the time is right.

Again, I'm not saying to avoid social situations or relationships with other singles. In fact, it's still true that "he who finds a wife finds a good thing" (Proverbs 18:22), which implies that a single man must make an effort to seek a wife if he wants to experience the benefits of marriage. What I'm talking about is the frantic kind of dating in which a single goes from one person to another, hoping one day to bump into the right one but often getting messed up in the search.

CONNECT WITH THE ONE WHO KNOWS WHERE THE RIGHT ONE IS

I'll never forget a single young woman in our church in Dallas who had it together. She was loving and serving God and minding her own business until one Sunday several years ago when she came to church alone because a friend who usually came with her couldn't make it.

This young woman was sitting in the second row of our family center, where we met for church in those days. A young man came into church that morning and looked for a seat in the back row, which was filled. The ushers escorted him to the front and seated him next to this woman. During the greeting time they said hello to each other— and you can guess the rest. They got married not long after that. It doesn't take long when God sets things up.

That won't happen for everybody, but whether it happens or not, God wants single people to seek Him, not seek a mate in the sense that you're on a mission that comes to dominate your decisions and your commitments. You don't need to find the right one. You need to connect with the One who knows where the right one is.

Singles who are waiting on God with the right kind of thinking know that marriage is not an escape from loneliness or lack of fulfillment or temptation, because there are lonely, unfulfilled, and tempted married people.

If you're thinking this way, God says change your mind. You're all right the way you are. Talk to God about your desires, but don't think there's something wrong with you that will never be fixed unless and until you get married.

WAIT WITH THE RIGHT VIEW OF MORTALITY

Waiting on the Lord also involves a proper understanding of your mortality. I'll let the Word explain what I mean:

> But this I say, brethren, the time has been shortened, so that from now on those who have wives should be as though they had none; and those who weep, as though they did not weep; and those who rejoice, as though they did not rejoice; and those who buy, as though they did not possess; and those who use the world, as though they did not make full use of it; for the form of this world is passing away. (1 Corinthians 7:29–31)

Life is too short, the apostle Paul says, to get all hung up on stuff—even relationships—that are going to pass away when God torches this present world and its system. Remember, God wants us to take the long, that is, the eternal, view of life. Anything that we can't send on ahead into heaven is strictly temporary and destined to pass away.

Paul illustrated his point with several earthly activities, but significantly that his first illustration is marriage. This is not a put-down on marriage, but a sober assessment of what counts most in life. Jesus said there will be no marriage in heaven because we will be like the angels, in the sense of being unmarried as they are (see Matthew 22:30).

In other words, marriage will pass away just like other earthly activities such as buying and selling. There is certainly nothing wrong with desiring to be married. Just don't treat marriage as if you'll die unhappy if you don't experience it. We as Christians can't afford to give anything on earth more time or weight than it deserves, or else it will start detracting from our eternal perspective.

"WAIT, JESUS. I'M NOT MARRIED YET"

One day while talking with a single man he told me, "I don't want Jesus to rapture me yet. He just needs to delay His coming a little longer because I'm not married yet."

Now he may have been kidding a little bit, but that's a pretty common view among singles. We've already established that there is nothing wrong with singles desiring a mate and developing relationships that could lead to marriage. But when any earthly goal overtakes a heavenly goal, we're vulnerable to making a mistake.

One mistake some Christian singles make when they elevate marriage to the top of their priority list is that they marry an unbeliever. We're going to talk later about what it means to be married "in the Lord" (1 Corinthians 7:39), so let me just mention this one for now because it's a big problem.

Bad things can happen when single people start fixating on marriage to the exclusion of other aspects of life. They begin to think that they're missing out on something good—or, worse, that God is holding out on them because He doesn't love them as much as the Bible says He does.

Singles in that situation are very vulnerable to the same deception that Satan worked on Eve in the garden of Eden. It was a masterful plan.

Let's say for the sake of illustration that there were one hundred trees in the garden. That meant Eve had ninety-nine beautiful trees to eat from freely, because God only put one tree off-limits: the Tree of the Knowledge of Good and Evil.

But you can read about Satan's strategy in Genesis 3. He got Eve to focus and fixate on that one forbidden tree. "G-i-r-r-l-l, you see that tree? Why would God keep that one tree from you if He loves you? He's holding out on you, because He knows that tree will make you be like Him."

What Satan tries to do with singles is put marriage or sex before them and tell them, "If God really cared about you, He wouldn't deprive you of these pleasures. After all, He created them for you. Go ahead and enjoy the fruit."

WHAT'S THE DIFFERENCE BETWEEN A SUCCESSFUL AND DEFEATED SINGLE?

Too many singles are so hung up on getting married that they never get around to enjoying the whole garden of opportunities and service that God has for them. That's the difference between a successful single and a defeated single.

Life is too short to focus all your energies on something that may last thirty or forty years as opposed to the things of God that will last forever.

Now don't misunderstand. It's fine to pray for a mate, desire a mate, and anticipate the day when you will have a mate. If you want to be married, assume that God is going to allow you to be married at some point unless He changes your desire.

But don't forget that He is also preparing you for greater things than just being married. Paul said he had the right to marry a believing woman (see 1 Corinthians 9:5), and no doubt he had thought about it. We tend to canonize and sterilize Paul and forget that he was a man with normal human desires. But Paul surrendered his right to marry for the greater calling of the kingdom of God. God doesn't call everyone to do that, but He does call us to "set [our] mind on the things above, not on the things that are on earth" (Colossians 3:2).

You can do this while you're waiting on the Lord for a husband or wife. You can do this once you're married. But you really can't set your mind on the things of heaven while your heart is fixated on the things of earth. As you wait on the Lord, don't lose your eternal focus. A proper focus will make the wait a lot easier.

2

WORKING FOR THE LORD

Now we're going to take this matter of being a Christian single person a little deeper, because God's viewpoint on singleness and marriage is different from the world's view, which we would expect. Unfortunately, God's view on singleness is also frequently different from the view singles are getting in the church, which should not be the case.

The world—and too often the church—treat singleness as an awkward, in-between stage from adolescence to marriage, a temporary stopover that tends to make singles feel like second-class citizens. But God views both singleness and marriage as *divine callings* in which we are to work for Him with all the commitment we can give.

To help you see this, I want to back up a bit in 1 Corinthians 7 and look at verses 20 and 24. Verse 20: "Each man must remain in that condition in which he was called." Verse 24: "Each one is to remain with God in that condition in which he was called."

These are two very important verses when it comes to the way your marital status relates to your calling as a Christian. The key in each verse is the word *condition*. In verse 20, this is actually the same Greek term as the word translated "called."

In other words, God is saying, "Remain in the calling to which you were called." This is significant because it equates our status as singles or marrieds with our calling. Verse 24 has the same idea because the word *condition* is in italics. That means it is not in the Greek text but was supplied by the translators. We could just as easily supply the word *calling* in verse 24 and get the proper sense of the passage.

HIS DIVINE CALLING

What I'm saying is that your calling as a single person is not just the current status you happen to be in. It is part of your divine calling.

The problem today is that many singles separate their status from their calling. This creates trouble because it can lead them to focus their energies on trying to change their marital status while missing their *present* calling as singles.

If you are single, your singleness is not just *where you happen to be* right now. It's *where God has you right now*, and there's a world of difference between those two outlooks.

Your singleness is part of your calling from the Lord, your reason for being, or your divinely ordained purpose. This doesn't mean you have to be in full-time Christian ministry. Your calling may involve serving as a physician or an accountant or whatever else for the glory and the kingdom of God. Once you see being single as a calling from God, you can give yourself to following and serving Him without anxiety about your future.

Have you ever thought about your single status as a calling? It is a divinely ordained state, not just a physical, relational state. God does not want you to reduce where He has you just because you want to be married. He wants you to hang out with Him in the state that you are in until—or if—He takes you to another calling.

Now, I know what many singles may be thinking at this point. They're afraid to accept singleness as a "calling" because it sounds like they're locking themselves into being unmarried the rest of their lives. But that's not necessarily true. God can alter your single status any time He chooses. The good news is that Christians can fulfill their calling whether they're single or married.

So what should you know in order to live victoriously as a single person while you work for the Lord? Let me give you three principles from God's Word.

GOD WANTS YOU TO BE FREE

As he urged believers in Corinth to stay in their call-ing, Paul told the singles that those who marry "will have trouble in this life, and I am trying to spare you" (1 Corinthians 7:28). Later he said, "I want you to be free from concern" (v. 32).

God wants singles to stop worrying and obsessing about when and whom they will marry. He wants them to enjoy the freedom their status gives them to serve Him without distractions.

This is so important that I want to make a statement that may catch you off-guard for a minute: *If you are a Christian single who is preoccupied with getting married to the point that you are frustrated day in and day out, week in and week out, then you are living outside the will of God.*

I say that because if this is true of you, you are living with a focus that God never meant you to have. God says you ought to be free from the distractions that marriage brings. Singles who are concentrating more on marriage than on living for God are like those who talk on a cell phone while they're driving. You risk an accident if you try to do both at the same time.

Let's get it straight. In the context of 1 Corinthians 7, singles are the free ones while married people are bound. Paul does speak of married people as being "bound" with no concept of "release" (v. 27). And freedom does mean liberty from bondage.

So single believers are to be free from concern. But

what concern? Paul explained further. "One who is unmarried is concerned about the things of the Lord, how he
may please the Lord; but one who is married is concerned
about the things of the world, how he may please his wife,
and his interests are divided" (1 Corinthians 7:32–34a).

The distinction Paul made is important. He was not
saying that married people don't care about pleasing the
Lord in terms of being the Christian He wants them to be.
God expects all believers to please Him regardless of marital status.

Instead, the idea of "pleasing the Lord" here has to do
with fulfilling our calling. In that sense, it's true that married people have more issues to be concerned about than
singles do. A single person can, for example, answer a call
to the mission field or accept a job in a different location
without having to check with anyone, or without having
to affect anyone else's plans.

A young woman in our church once told me she was
going to the mission field for a period of service while she
had the opportunity. "Pastor," she said, "I may not be able
to do this later if I get married."

Obviously, married people have their mates to consider in such decisions. And sometimes the task of blend-
ing two people with different personalities and ideas can
produce a tension that every married couple has felt. As
we saw earlier, Paul passed up his right to get married for
the sake of his calling.

Single Christian, don't sacrifice the freedom you have
by acting like a married person. What I mean is some sin-

gles are so hung up on being married that they basically put themselves in the same situation as married people. That is, their attention is already as divided as if they were married, so they aren't truly fulfilling their calling as singles. They're free, but living as if they're bound.

When two people come together as one in marriage, they give up their right to act independently. The fact that they now have another person to care for also means that married couples must increase their focus on everyday needs and concerns, which Paul called "the things of the world" (vv. 33–34).

> # THE RIGHT PERSPECTIVE IS TO SEE SINGLENESS AS AN ADVANTAGE FROM A KINGDOM PERSPECTIVE.

That's not a condemnation, but rather recognition of the fact that marriage requires a lot of time, commitment, and resources. The difference is between an earthly perspective and an eternal perspective. Desiring to be married is a noble desire, but God wants to make sure that Christians go into marriage with their eyes open to its demands, and not to seek marriage at the cost of their commitment to Him and their calling from Him.

The person who has the right perspective sees single-ness as an advantage, not a disadvantage. It's an advantage from a kingdom perspective, not because marriage as its intended institution is bad but because it is distracting, sometimes disappointing, and brings with it concerns that a single person does not have. One lady once said to me at church, "Pastor, I wish someone would have told me before I got married that marriage 'ain't all that.'"

What the world, the media, entertainment, music, and often even your friends and relatives try to do is make a bigger deal out of marriage than even God makes out of it. God's value system states clearly that if you are the right kind of single with an eternal perspective, than you are just fine. You are not a second rate citizen, and in fact you might not be missing out on anything at all. You might be saving yourself from a lifetime of boredom and trouble.

Being unmarried offers single people an unusual de-gree of freedom to not only pursue God's calling for their lives, but to pursue the passions that make a person feel alive. A single person has the opportunity to explore hid-den talents, take risks to achieve things they dream about, and experience things they could never experience were they married. But that means Christian singles have a de-cision to make—whether to focus on who God made them to be, or spend their time worrying about when Mr. or Miss Right is going to show up.

The biblical heroine Ruth is a great example of a sin-gle person who made the right decision. Ruth was a widow living in her native Moab with two other widows: her sister-in-law, Orpah, and her mother-in-law, Naomi, who had moved to Moab from Bethlehem.

If you're familiar with the story from the book of Ruth, you know that Naomi decided to go back to Israel and tried to send her daughters-in-law Ruth and Orpah back to their families in Moab because the chances of these widows finding husbands in Israel were slim.

Orpah listened to Naomi and went back to her pagan people, but Ruth had another agenda. She had become a believer in the God of Israel, and she was determined to follow Him. That meant following Naomi back to Bethlehem even if it meant that Ruth would never marry again.

> RUTH WAS DETERMINED TO FOLLOW GOD EVEN IF IT MEANT THAT SHE WOULD NEVER MARRY AGAIN.

Now we know that God had a husband in mind for Ruth, but she didn't know that. She just wanted to serve God and take care of Naomi, which we could say was Ruth's calling from God.

Ruth made a spiritual decision, a theological choice based on her love for God, whereas Orpah made a social decision. Orpah disappeared from the scene, while Ruth became famous in Israel. We'll look at her story in more detail in chapter 3.

The interesting thing is that Naomi the Israelite, who knew the true God, was more interested in trying to get Ruth and Orpah married off than she was in trying to encourage them to become true followers of God.

But Ruth had enough sense to understand that her calling from God superseded her marital status. Ruth freely decided to go back to Bethlehem with Naomi, even though, as far as she knew, as a foreigner only poverty and singleness awaited her. At that point Ruth was truly free to follow God, and God was free to work miraculously in her life.

Too many Christian singles are listening to too many Naomis, who are trying to get them married off instead of encouraging them to fulfill their divine calling. God wants you to be free in your singleness, so don't let other people set your agenda or try to rush you into marriage.

GOD WANTS YOU TO FUNCTION

God not only wants you to be free as a single person, but He wants you to use that freedom to function for His kingdom. God wants single believers to be set apart for His service.

Being set apart is the basic meaning of the word *holy*, as Paul wrote in 1 Corinthians 7:34: "The woman who is unmarried, and the virgin, is concerned about the things of the Lord, that she may be holy both in body and spirit."

Now again, don't misunderstand. Every believer is to be set apart for God's service, and married Christians are also called to be holy in body and spirit. But Paul was emphasizing the unique opportunity that unmarried people have to focus their time and energies on serving the Lord.

One of the great historical examples of a person being set apart for service, outside of Jesus Christ, of course, is Queen Elizabeth I of England. Queen Elizabeth rose to the throne when she was only twenty-four years old. Her father, Henry VIII, had served as king with a tumultuous reign that saw the beheading of not only Elizabeth's mother, but another of his wives as well.

When Elizabeth attained to her rightful place as queen, following the death of her half-sister, Queen Mary I, she made a purposeful decision to remain single. Despite multiple efforts of advisors from within and royal leaders from without to connect her in a marriage of political convenience, Elizabeth stood her ground. In fact, one time when Parliament was pushing to persuade her yet again to get married and bear an heir to the throne, Elizabeth replied stately, "I have already joined myself in marriage to a husband, namely the kingdom of England."

Well aware of her own personal convictions, power, and influence, and how that may become jeopardized by a marriage, Elizabeth embraced not only her singlehood but also her celibacy. She is also recorded as having said to Parliament, "It would please me best if, at the last, a marble stone shall record that this queen having lived such and such a time, lived and died a virgin."

QUEEN ELIZABETH EMBRACED NOT ONLY HER SINGLEHOOD BUT ALSO HER CELIBACY.

Elizabeth's queenly reign in the kingdom lasted forty-four years, at a time when the reign of kings or queens could sometimes last less than a year, and certainly usually no more than ten. Hers was an age where England prospered not only financially but spiritually, socially, and creatively. The time of her rule is best known as the Elizabethan era, or the Golden Age. Her singular dedication to the betterment of her kingdom produced some of the greatest advancements for her people that they had seen in hundreds of years.

Not only was Queen Elizabeth I the wife of her kingdom, but she was also the mother of its people, having said to Parliament, "Though after my death you may have many stepdames, yet shall you never have a more natural mother unto you all." Queen Elizabeth I used her freedom from marriage to fully maximize not only her life on earth, but the lives of countless others.

Single Christians need to answer the question of how well they are using their unique freedom to function in a way that contributes to God's kingdom as well. Is there a direct correlation between what you do every day and the calling you have to fulfill God's purpose for you? Or are you allowing the world to distract you from your divine calling and function?

Whenever I teach on this, I think of the story that was told about Yogi Berra, the great catcher for the New York Yankees, and Hank Aaron, baseball's all-time home-run king.

The story goes that as Aaron came to bat in the All-Star Game one time, Berra did all he could to distract the great slugger. Berra was a chatterbox behind the plate, always trying to distract the hitters, so he said to Aaron, "Hey Hank, you're holding your bat the wrong way. You should have the label turned up so you can read it." But Aaron ignored Berra and said nothing.

> # DON'T LET OTHER PEOPLE DISTRACT YOU FROM YOUR CALLING.

Yogi wouldn't give up, however. "Hank, I'm telling you, you're holding the bat the wrong way. The label should be turned where you can read it." But still Aaron said nothing.

After this had gone on for several pitches, Aaron suddenly hit the next pitch out of the park for a home run. As he crossed home plate, he said to Berra, "Yogi, I came up here to hit, not to read."

You and I need to know why we are here. We need to say, "I came here to hit home runs." Don't let other people distract you from your calling, or you'll be standing at home plate messing with the bat instead of swinging for the fences.

Like home-run king Hank Aaron, the first man Adam focused on his calling. What was Adam doing when he found a wife? He wasn't out girl-watching, because there were no other human beings around. He wasn't daydreaming about his wedding day. Adam was busy functioning in his God-given role of tending the Garden of Eden and, more specifically, naming the animals when God put him to sleep and removed a rib to fashion Eve (see Genesis 2:19–22).

Notice that as Adam functioned in his calling, God used that situation to create the scenario in which He itroduced Adam to his mate. As Adam named each animal he noticed that, for example, for every Mr. Leopard there was a Mrs. Leopard. In other words, every animal had its mate. But there was no one who corresponded to Adam.

So by the time Adam had finished naming the animals,

it was abundantly clear that there was no one for him. The Bible even says, "But for Adam there was not found a helper suitable for him" (Genesis 2:20). By the time Adam had finished his work and noticed his need, God was ready to supply him with a mate.

God does not want you sitting around so focused on your wedding day that you miss out on the pleasures and purpose that He has for you today. He wants you functioning for Him until, or even if, He creates your wedding day.

Too many singles are like people going for a Sunday drive. My parents used to take me and my siblings for Sunday drives in the afternoon. The goal was just to go, not to go anywhere in particular. That was fun for a while, but then it became boring.

Are you going through life aimlessly, or do you have a mission and a sense of calling on your life? Do you have a passion from God that motivates you? If you are a single Christian, it's because God has you single, and you ought to know why He wants you to function in this calling for whatever period He deems right.

It's easy to get consumed in endless activity that doesn't take you anywhere. Single people have a unique freedom to find and pursue God's purpose for them and to function in that calling with undivided, undistracted commitment to Christ.

GOD WANTS TO CHANGE YOUR FOCUS

Living freely and fully for Christ as an unmarried believer will require a change of your focus from being preoccupied with marriage to being preoccupied with Jesus.

Paul wrote in verse 35, "This I say for your own benefit; not to put a restraint upon you, but to promote what is appropriate and to secure undistracted devotion to the Lord." The only way to avoid distractions is to keep your focus in the right place.

Paul was not trying to put handcuffs on single Christians and keep the two sexes apart. He wasn't trying to prevent people from desiring to get married or pursuing matrimony. He was not anti-marriage at all. But there was a benefit in being single that Paul wanted to make sure his readers understood.

We've been talking about this benefit, which is stated here as "undistracted devotion to the Lord." One way Satan robs us of God's best is to cause a disturbance in our lives to distract us, much the way one thief may distract a store clerk so the other thief can steal merchandise or money without being noticed.

Satan has so many Christian singles so disturbed and worried about their marital status that he's running amok through their lives, stealing their joy and robbing them of their effectiveness for Christ. When your focus shifts from Christ to yourself, that means a thief is at work on you.

Paul's point in this passage is that those married, by

virtue of being husband and wife, have divided loyalties. They need to please their spouse, fulfill their own purpose, as well as please God. They are constantly going back and forth among these focuses because the very nature of the relationships forces the division.

But a Christian single is undivided. Yet one of the reasons why there are so many frustrated singles today is that they are experiencing as a single what they should only be experiencing if they were married. The result is they feel divided. By being consumed with thoughts about marriage, dating, and finding a mate, many singles live under the strain of divided loyalties. If God hasn't given you a mate to worry about yet, then my advice to you is to leave that person alone in your priorities, time, and thoughts. Because that person doesn't exist yet.

> A SUCCESSFUL SINGLE MAXIMIZES HER SINGLEHOOD FOR THE BETTERMENT OF OTHERS AND THE ADVANCEMENT OF GOD'S KINGDOM.

The moment that you are divided emotionally and spiritually, you have let your singlehood get in the way of

God's kingdom purpose for your life and well-being. If you are spending an inordinate amount of your time thinking about marriage, looking at wedding dresses, watching television programs about people getting married—or who are married—and as a result feeling frustrated and distracted, then you have been pulled off course of a spiritual focus.

A successful single is one who maximizes his or her singlehood for the betterment of others, the advancement of God's kingdom, and the manifestation of His glory.

When God made Adam, Adam didn't have a wife. He was single and satisfied. It wasn't Adam who said, "I'm lonely, let God make a mate suitable for me." It was God who noticed that Adam would fulfill his specific purpose better through the addition of Eve. Yet Adam was totally occupied with God's purposes, living as a fulfilled individual. He wasn't distracted from his job of naming things and carrying out his role in God's establishment of earth.

Here is the question that every single man and woman should ask: "God, how do You want me to use the state that I am in until You change my state for Your maximum purpose?" When God answers that question—even though the desire to be married may still remain—you will have a passion and a purpose that will supersede any dominating thoughts you once held for marriage.

It is easy to become distracted by unhealthy relationships, television programs, and even personal discouragement. However, God is trying to get your attention so that you can experience all the fullness that He has in store for you in this phase of your life. It is during this time of singlehood that you should be preparing yourself emotionally and spiritually in order to become the best you that you can be. You don't just want to avoid marrying the wrong person someday; you want to avoid *being* the wrong person when or if you do get married. That requires time to focus on the race that God has mapped out for your own personal spiritual growth.

AN UNDISTRACTED FOCUS

Several years ago the Goodwill Games, an international track and field competition, were being held in Edmonton, Canada. During the four-by-one-hundred relay, a Jamaican athlete who was to run the third leg of the race for his team allowed his attention to wander as he waited for the baton to be passed.

This usually focused runner happened to look up at the big screen that was televising another event and saw a friend of his getting ready to compete. The runner stared at the screen for just a few seconds, but as he did so his teammate came running up to him with the baton. Instead of a smooth handoff, the incoming runner collided with his distracted teammate, and the race was over for the Jamaican team.

The message for us is clear. We need to stop looking at other people's races and start running our own race. For singles, this includes keeping your focus on God instead of always looking around trying to find a partner. God is saying to single believers, "Focus on Me, and I will do your looking for you."

If you live in a large metropolitan where the roads often seem to be under construction or clogged with traffic, you learn that it doesn't pay to go very far without tuning in to the latest traffic report. In Dallas where I live, the traffic updates often include a helicopter reporter, who can see beyond the traffic tie-ups on the ground and give drivers the big picture, including warnings of trouble ahead and alternate routes. When you are tuned in to a helicopter reporter, you hear things that other busy drivers don't get to hear.

The same is true if you pull up a traffic app on your smartphone and glance at it when you come to a stop in traffic. You receive a different, more comprehensive view showing where the traffic is the most congested on the roads that you are seeking to travel on.

That's what focusing on the Lord does for believers. When you are tuned in to the Lord in terms of undivided devotion to Him, you'll hear things and see things that other people won't hear or see because your heart is listening to Him.

I love the story of the businessman and the Native American who were walking down a noisy street in the city one day. Suddenly, the Native American stopped and said, "Shhh. Listen!"

The businessman said, "Listen for what?"

"Don't you hear it?" the Native American asked. "It's a cricket."

The businessman said, "A cricket? I don't hear anything."

But the Native American looked around and saw a cricket on the sidewalk. He reached down, picked it up, and showed it to the businessman, who was amazed. "I don't believe it. Here we are downtown with all this noise and all these people, and you hear a cricket. How did you do that?"

"I'll show you," the other man said. He took some change out of his pocket and threw it on the sidewalk. As the money clattered and rolled around, twenty people stopped to look. "You always hear what you're tuned to hear," the Native American said.

> BE TUNED IN TO GOD. REMEMBER,
> HE'S THE ONLY ONE WHO
> KNOWS HOW TO GET ADAM
> AND EVE TOGETHER.

A lot of singles will never find their mate because they're tuned to their friends or the dating scene or something else instead of being tuned in to God. But He's the only One who knows how to get Adam and Eve together.

Single Christian, if you will set your focus on God and function for Him in the freedom He has given you, you won't have to worry about Him finding you when He's ready to link you with someone. Look to God, and let Him do your looking for you.

One day way back before the days of cell phones and texting, I was at the airport trying to get to my gate for the flight out when I heard my name announced over the intercom: "Dr. Tony Evans, please go to the nearest white courtesy phone for a message."

Now I was concentrating on something else because I had a flight to make and a destination to reach, so it took a few seconds for the reality to sink in that I was the one being paged. I went to the nearest phone and received a message from my assistant, Sylvia, who needed to contact me and knew I was still at the airport because she makes my travel arrangements.

How did this phone call find me in the middle of thousands of people who also had flights to make and plans to keep? I was doing what I was called to do, on my way to minister the Word of God to people. I didn't go to the airport to hang out and wait for a call from Sylvia.

But when she needed to reach me, it was no problem because she knew where I was and because the airport has a system in place to reach travelers with important messages. And the fact that I was immersed in a sea of people in the middle of a noisy terminal was no obstacle at all.

God may send you to an airport because He wants to take you somewhere and has a plan in mind to get you there. And when you as a single Christian decide that you are going to focus on Christ and His plan for you, if God wants to interrupt your plans and call your name with a message, He knows how to reach you. He knows how to reroute you. He can track you down, call you by name, and set you off in an entirely different direction than you ever even knew was possible.

In the meantime, your job is to keep your focus on the Lord and keep moving ahead with His plan for you. Once you're ready to fly high with the Lord, He is freed up to make a connection with you and for you.

3

WEDDED IN
THE LORD

Obviously being single could be for just a season of your life. Marriage may be part of God's plans for you. So as we conclude, here are some essential principles single believers need to practice as they consider a possible marriage in their future.

It's safe to assume that the majority of single people hope and expect to be married someday. It's true that more women than in the past are able to have satisfying careers, earn a significant income, and experience the freedoms previously denied or limited to them, which has brought about a rise in the choice of singlehood in our nation. Yet many women—and working men too—still desire to be married.

That's good, because God created marriage and holds

it in high esteem. But as I have pointed out, the Bible also makes it clear that those who are not married have not somehow fallen into a second-class-citizen status in the kingdom.

In 1 Corinthians 7, Paul's great chapter on singleness and marriage, he concluded by dealing with the case of a single person who desires to get married (vv. 36–40). This person may have never been married, or may be single again after a divorce or the death of a spouse. No doubt you fit in one of these three categories if you are unmarried. I call these three categories those who are single, those who wish they were single, and those who are single again.

The apostle has some helpful instructions for each of these single men and women—and along the way Paul even adds a special word to people who are now married.

A WORD TO THE SINGLE

The first category of singleness Paul addressed is those who have never been married. "If any man thinks that he is acting unbecomingly toward his virgin daughter, if she is past her youth, and if it must be so, let him do what he wishes, he does not sin; let her marry" (1 Corinthians 7:36).

This is a message to fathers whose single daughters are feeling their biological clock ticking and want to get married. A father in this case is not to try to prevent his daughter's marriage. Now this assumes that the father has had input into the choice of a potential marriage partner, a major point we'll deal with in a minute.

Before we move to that, notice verses 37–38, which answer the question of what happens when a single woman is content to remain so and the father thinks this is the best option: "But he who stands firm in his heart, being under no constraint, but has authority over his own will, and has decided this in his own heart, to keep his own virgin *daughter*, he will do well. So then both he who gives his own virgin daughter in marriage does well, and he who does not give her in marriage will do better."

What is interesting about this passage is that in your Bible, the word "daughter" should be italicized. This is because it did not appear in the original text. Translators later added it in order to try and make the sentence more understandable in the English language. Yet if you leave the word "daughter" out altogether, it would read, "to keep his own virgin." In that case, it could equally refer to a relational situation between a man and a woman. By that I mean that if a man and a woman are in a relationship that is starting to get heated sexually—and yet they are not yet married—the man needs to marry her or break up with her, because the thing that he is not to do is mess over her. A man should never jeopardize a woman's honor just to have a relationship with her.

With the word "daughter" in the passage, this case presupposes that the daughter is also content to remain single, since it's hard to imagine a caring father refusing to honor his daughter's legitimate desires to get married and deciding to keep her single against her wishes. A woman who is not worried about getting married shouldn't be pressured by others because singleness is a perfectly acceptable choice—and even "better" in the context of being free to serve Christ.

But we're assuming the case of a single person who desires to get married. When Paul talked about a father who "gives" his daughter in marriage, he had a lot more in mind than we normally think of.

In today's culture, a father sometimes doesn't even meet his daughter's future husband until the two are already serious, and then dad's job is limited to paying the wedding bills and walking his daughter down the aisle to answer the preacher's question, "Who gives this woman to be married to this man?"

Things were radically different in biblical days. Paul was writing in a context in which marriages were typically arranged by the parents. In the biblical world, there was no thought that parents would not be involved in the marriage of their children.

That's because the family was viewed as a continuum from one generation to another, not as a bunch of isolated units who happened to be related. The continuation and well-being of the family was in part dependent on how successful each generation was in establishing solid marriages and homes.

And so if a daughter in this context wanted to get married, her father was to get involved in the process of selecting and approving a potential mate. There's a lot here to deal with, and you may already be raising questions, so stay with me. I think the following discussion will deal with the pertinent issues.

First of all, as we saw earlier, the Bible tells singles not to be wife- or husband-hunting (see 1 Corinthians 7:27). This doesn't mean a single person can't meet others and establish relationships. The idea is not to buy into the world's mentality that there's something wrong if you're not married, or depend on the world's methods of finding a mate.

> # A YOUNG WOMAN'S FATHER CAN EVALUATE A POSSIBLE HUSBAND'S FITNESS AND DISCERN THE DIRECTION AND POTENTIAL OF HIS LIFE.

So if a woman wants to get married, whom should she tell first of all? Her father, because he is to be actively involved in the process.

Why? For a number of reasons. A young woman's father is, or should be, the one man in her life who has her deepest interests at heart, who has been given the responsibility of being her spiritual leader, and who is in the position to evaluate a possible husband's fitness from a man's perspective and discern the direction and potential of his life.

Now you may be saying, "Come on, Tony, you're not saying we should go back to arranged marriages, are you? This is the twenty-first century, not the first century."

Well, my answer to that question depends on what is meant by arranged marriages. If we're talking about cases in which two fathers, or two sets of parents, get together and pledge their children to each other before the two have met or have even grown up, that's not going to happen in our culture (although it still happens in other countries). But if we are talking about serious parental involvement and approval in the mate-selection process, then yes, this is the norm that the Bible teaches.

Some would say that this was no more than a social custom the way they did it in Paul's day. But this is not the case. The principle of a father giving his daughter in marriage, in the biblical sense of preparing her for that marriage, was laid down at the first marriage when God created Eve and "brought her" to Adam (Genesis 2:22).

God the Father walked Eve down the aisle, so to speak, and presented her to Adam, establishing the pattern that we still use in marriage ceremonies today. I'd like to suggest this is a theological matter and not merely a social custom. The Father approved his daughter's marriage and then validated it by giving her away.

In fact, I believe that every unmarried woman ought to have a male looking out for her marital interests. Ideally, that should be her father. But many fathers are absent today, and some others who are present are either not believers or are not spiritually attuned.

In cases where believing women do not have a father who can fill that role, the church is to act as a father and look after their spiritual and marital interests. The Bible speaks of the church leaders as fathers among the body of Christ (see 1 Corinthians 4:14–15; 1 Thessalonians 2:11).

> # SIMILARLY, A YOUNG MAN WHO HAS A GODLY FATHER AND MOTHER WOULD DO WELL TO HEED THEIR ADVICE.

What happens when the single person in question is a son and not a daughter? Many of the same principles apply, because sons also need to benefit from the wisdom and instruction of their parents. The New Testament doesn't address this issue directly as it does for women, but clearly a young man who has a godly father and mother would do well to heed their advice and follow their spiritual leadership.

Of course, arranged marriages in biblical days did

involve sons. The classic example is Abraham sending his servant to find a bride for Isaac (Genesis 24:1–4)—in this case a young woman named Rebekah whom Isaac didn't even meet until the marriage had been arranged.

Since we're dealing with single women in the text before us in 1 Corinthians 7, let's talk about a father's role in helping his daughter to marry in the Lord. One reason for a father's involvement is to make sure that his daughter doesn't marry a man who turns out to be a fool.

A younger person may be swayed by the externals, by the front that the other person puts up. But a father who is walking with the Lord can help his daughter see the real deal in a potential husband, and he can demand some serious commitments from the man who desires to marry his daughter.

When I married my wife, Lois, her father had me write a letter outlining my basic commitments, and he still has it on file. My two sons-in-law had to write similar letters, which are in my file. We had to have some meetings and come to some basic agreements before they married my daughters.

Single Christian woman, if you have a father who walks with the Lord and you are thinking about marrying someone your father doesn't agree with, you are taking a massive risk. If you and your dad are on the same page spiritually and are committed to the Lord, then God will validate your marital choice through your father.

With women's full entry into the workforce and more people waiting longer to get married, many single women today are successfully established on their own. Sometimes a woman in this position will meet a man who doesn't have a regular job, drives an old beat-up car, and is still living with his mama.

Now what this woman doesn't need is someone who will take her backward, or a guy who is only looking for someone to pay all of his bills. So there needs to be some evaluation of his situation, and a father can help his daughter measure this man's potential and his spiritual condition.

For example, maybe this man isn't where he wants to be right now, but he's showing signs of moving in the right direction. He may be in college working toward a degree, or he's having to overcome some hard circumstances. A woman needs her father to help her evaluate a potential husband objectively because if she is in love with the guy, she may not see all of these things or may overlook some red flags.

A father is in a good position to evaluate marriage potential because he knows what is involved in fulfilling the biblical instruction for a man to leave his father and mother and cleave to his wife.

The Bible only speaks of a woman leaving her parents in respect to the man leaving his parents (Genesis 2:24). The reason is that a woman is always to be covered and protected by authority. She is to be covered by her biological father, or a spiritual substitute, until such time as she is given away in marriage to a man who is pledged to cover and protect her. A woman who desires to be married needs to take seriously the Bible's admonition to follow God's order and line of authority through her father.

A WORD TO THOSE WHO WISH THEY WERE SINGLE

We also need to address another group of people— those who aren't single, but wish they were. These are people who say they didn't realize what they were getting into when they got married, and now they want out. The unfortunate fact is that plenty of married people wish they were single again.

These may be cases in which it is better to be single than to be married. It's better to be single wanting to be married than it is to be married wanting to be single. You can change your single status, but you aren't to undo a marriage simply because you want out.

Once you're married you are bound to your mate for life. Paul stated an important principle of marriage when he wrote, "A wife is bound as long as her husband lives" (1 Corinthians 7:39a). We've talked about the bondage of marriage versus the freedom of singleness, so we won't go there again.

People need to understand what they are agreeing to when they say, "I do," because too many married people *don't* anymore. Both partners in a marriage are bound to each other as long as they both live, because the principle works both ways. Marriage is easy to get into, but hard to get out of because you are bound.

Now I know we have no-fault divorce today. Society

may recognize divorce for incompatibility or irreconcilable differences, but God doesn't recognize either of these reasons. So although the judge downtown may declare you divorced in such cases, in God's eyes you are still married.

God hates divorce (Malachi 2:16). The only conditions that may permit divorce are adultery or abandonment (See Matthew 5:31–32, 19:9; 1 Corinthians 7:15). Even then, one can forgive an unfaithful spouse who repents, and the marriage relationship may be restored. (In cases of abuse, a separation may be necessary for the safety of the mistreated spouse, with the hope that the abuser, through counsel, can change and the marriage eventually be restored.) God also permits divorce in the case of spiritual death, discussed in the next section.

> ## SOCIETY MAY RECOGNIZE DIVORCE FOR IRRECONCILABLE DIFFERENCES, BUT GOD DOESN'T.

A single person may say, "Hey, you're scaring me about getting married." Good! If you're single, you'd better be sober-minded and a little scared about making this commitment, because once you're married you are bound to your mate for life.

Jesus once delivered some straight teaching on marriage and divorce in which He said that contrary to the popular view, it wasn't okay for a man to divorce his wife for any reason.

When Jesus was finished, His disciples said, "If the relationship of the man with his wife is like this, it is better not to marry" (Matthew 19:10). In other words, Jesus had scared them about being married, and He didn't back off. We need to do some serious and sober thinking about singleness and marriage.

A WORD TO THOSE WHO ARE SINGLE AGAIN

Paul continues in 1 Corinthians 7:39: "But if her husband is dead, she is free to be married to whom she wishes, only in the Lord." To close our study on singleness, we need to discuss the case of those who were once married and are now single again.

The Bible only grants freedom from a marriage for adultery, abandonment, or when the death of a spouse occurs. Now the Bible recognizes two kinds of death that can end a marriage. The first and most obvious is physical death, which clearly sets the living partner free from the marriage. In that instance, there is no disagreement that the marriage covenant has ended.

In addition there can be a spiritual death of the marriage. When God warned Adam not to eat from the forbidden tree, He said, "In the day that you eat from it you will surely die" (Genesis 2:17). Now the day Adam and Eve ate of the fruit, they did not drop dead physically, but they did die spiritually, and their relationship with God was broken.

The Bible recognizes the reality of spiritual death and the separation that it brings in a relationship. Jesus said divorce was wrong "except for immorality" (Matthew 19:9), which brings death to a marriage. The Bible says that when there is sexual immorality, which is a form of spiritual death, the marriage dies. There can be forgiveness and restoration, but immorality clearly introduces spiritual death into a marriage.

But the Word does not limit spiritual death to immorality within a marriage. On a broader scale it can include any lifestyle by any Christian that is contrary to the truth and detrimental to the kingdom of God. One example is found in 1 Corinthians 5:11, where Paul mentioned such things as drunkenness and swindling people.

So how can it be determined if a marriage is dead and a divorce can be granted without violating God's Word? The death must be recognized by the church, which pronounces that the union is dead and issues the death certificate. In the case of the incestuous man in 1 Corinthians 6, the church should have judged him because the church is God's court and God's coroner to determine if a death has occurred.

The point of 1 Corinthians 6 is that the church should act on God's behalf in matters that we normally take to the judge downtown. The church court should be a believer's first court of appeal in a dispute. If a married person believes that his or her marriage is spiritually dead, that person should appeal to the church for a judgment. Our church in Dallas holds a church court every week to deal with matters that come up.

In the case of marriage and divorce, the problem is that many people don't want to go to the church court because it's too tough. They want to go downtown, where it's easy to get a divorce. But God doesn't recognize a divorce until the church recognizes that spiritual death exists in the marriage, that one partner has been unfaithful or has developed a totally rebellious, unrepentant attitude.

I realize this is more involved than we can discuss fully in this brief context. But I want you to see that it takes death to dissolve a marriage and set a married person free to marry again.

You may be wondering why this is such a big deal. Let me encourage you to read Malachi 2:14–16, in which God told the people of Israel He hated divorce and that because they were divorcing their mates illegitimately He would not hear their prayers. Anyone who divorces for the wrong reasons leaves God standing at the altar too, because He says He won't listen to them.

But when a death has occurred in the marriage, the remaining spouse is free to remarry "in the Lord." There is freedom of choice within that boundary.

> # A BELIEVER AND AN UNBELIEVER ARE NEVER TO BE JOINED IN ANY CLOSE COEQUAL PARTNERSHIP, INCLUDING MARRIAGE.

What does it mean to be married in the Lord? Two concepts are at work here. The first is the stipulation that the person being considered for marriage needs to be a Christian. A believer and an unbeliever are never to be joined together in any close coequal partnership, including marriage.

Paul warned in 2 Corinthians 6:14–15, "Do not be bound together with unbelievers; for what partnership have righteousness and lawlessness, or what fellowship has light with darkness? Or what harmony has Christ with Belial, or what has a believer in common with an unbeliever?"

This concept actually comes from Deuteronomy 22:10, where God told Israel not to put an ox and a donkey together in the same yoke because they are different animals that won't be pulling together. They were not created to work together.

This is the picture of a Christian and a non-Christian

joining together in marriage. They will not be pulling together equally, and they are going to have problems.

A single man was at the airport one day when he met
a nice woman. They began talking and really began to
click with each other. Something was happening; a fire
was starting to ignite.

Finally the man asked the woman where she was flying to. It turned out she was flying north to Canada, while
he was flying south to Mexico. He wanted the two of
them to fly together, but it was impossible because they
were going in opposite directions.

If you're a Christian you are heading in the opposite
direction from an unbeliever, and the two of you can't be
yoked together without someone getting hurt. This is one
area where far too many Christian singles are willing to
compromise in order to get married. But the Bible forbids
marriage between a believer and a lost person under any
circumstance. Someone has said that if you marry a child
of the devil, you're going to have in-law problems.

YOU ARE NOT TO SEARCH
FOR A "SOUL MATE." YOU ARE TO
BE LOOKING FOR A "SPIRIT MATE."

To be married "only in the Lord" means that you are not supposed to marry an unbeliever. Now, people today talk about their search for their "soul mates." Keep in mind that is not the first mate you are supposed to be looking for. You are supposed to be looking for a *"spirit mate."* Deuteronomy 22:10 gives us some insight, "You shall not plow with an ox and a donkey together." The reason you don't put an ox and a donkey together with the same plow is that they won't pull together. They are two different types of animals. A spirit mate is someone who has the same goals and purpose as you do spiritually. This is the only thing that will keep a marriage together successfully over time. Because when the bodies get old and the souls wind up in conflict, you had better have the spirit left to hang onto. If that's not there, then nothing will keep you together.

The idea of marrying in the Lord and being equally joined with another Christian also has a deeper facet to it than just two people being saved and going to church. You should not only marry a Christian, but a Christian who is pulling in the same direction as you.

It's one thing to get married to a Christian, but it's another thing to marry a Christian whose spiritual desires and commitments complement yours instead of contradicting them.

For example, if you are committed to grow in your faith and you're moving in that direction, you are going to want someone who wants to grow in Christ too.

Earlier we used the example of a single person who

feels called to the mission field. If you have such a desire, and you meet another Christian who has no inkling at all that God is calling him or her to the mission field, this difference ought to cause the two of you to go very slowly in your relationship. Otherwise, you may wind up pulling in different directions.

This doesn't mean that two people who want to get married must be alike in everything. That will never happen in the first place, and if it did they would be in for a very boring relationship. But it's important that their differences are at least in the same direction.

So the desire for marriage is legitimate. But Paul concluded his extended teaching on this subject by saying, "In my opinion she [a widow] is happier if she remains as she is; and I think that I also have the Spirit of God" (1 Corinthians 7:40). This was not just a human opinion, but the revealed Word and will of God. In other words, Paul wasn't just telling his personal bias, but was speaking under the Spirit's inspiration.

Under the Spirit's direction, Paul literally states that a woman is "happier" if she remains single. Essentially, he says, "If she wants to get married, fine—that's her call. But only if she marries in the Lord. Keep in mind, though, she is going to be happier if she stays single."

Ladies, understand that if you want to get married you are actually giving up some happiness. If you could spend only a moment listening in on what so many married couples go through just on the ride home from church, you would think twice about wanting to get married. Sure, they might look all lovey-dovey dressed up in church praising the Lord, but sometimes the bickering and the fussing starts as early as reaching the pavement of the parking lot.

I'm not saying that there is anything wrong with getting married. I'm just saying that Paul, inspired by the Holy Spirit, said you will be happier if you don't. As a single, you are not in a lesser position. You are in a higher position. You are not in the reduced position. You are in the spiritually exalted position. Why do you think divorce rates are so high and have always been an issue throughout all time? Because married people realize they had it much better off when they were single.

WHY HURRY?

Single Christian—widow, widower, never married, or divorced—my counsel to you is don't be in a hurry to get married. Don't rush the process, and don't rush off to the altar with someone who may not be God's choice simply because you're afraid you may not get another chance. Don't be in such a hurry that you crash and burn.

Let me remind you again of Ruth, who was a widow and successful. Ruth determined to pursue God, even if it meant giving up the legitimate pursuit of a husband and the security of marriage.

Ruth went back to Israel with Naomi, assuming she would never get married again because she was a foreigner from Moab. But as she fulfilled her calling and served the Lord, the day came when she happened to glean in the fields of Boaz—and one of the Bible's great love stories began to unfold.

Ruth was in an obscure position, and humanly speaking was about as far from having marriage prospects as any woman in her day. But when God was ready, He found her, or rather, He made sure that Boaz found her.

But let me point out that the story of Ruth is not the story of a single woman getting married. It is the story of two people who were used of God to carry on the line of the Messiah. Obed, the son born to Ruth and Boaz, was the father of Jesse, who was the father of David, through whom came Jesus Christ!

God may have you single right now, but He may be preparing you for something that is much bigger than you could imagine!

YOUR THREE CHOICES

Let me give you a helpful formula for approaching single life. As a single Christian, you have three choices. Your first choice is to *grumble* about your lot and the lack of suitable potential mates and grumble that you aren't married because you can feel your biological clock ticking.

A second choice is to *grab* the next available person who comes along, regardless of that person's fitness for marriage. That's a bad choice, as we have seen.

A third choice for you as a Christian single is to *grow* in grace and in your walk with the Lord. You can say to

God, "I am going to walk with You no matter what, and I am going to trust You and wait on You for Your timing in my life."

What will your choice be? Make sure you make your choice based on your true value and worth because only then will you be making the right choice.

A man one day was shopping at an antique store where the owner, a woman, had a beautiful table for sale. The price on the table was $600, yet the man thought he would try and get a deal so he offered her $400. They began having a conversation about the table, and she informed him that she wouldn't take less than the asking price for this table. The man continued to ask for the discounted price, so the owner began telling him all of the unique qualities about this particular table.

Their conversation continued for some time, and then the man asked if she would be willing to take $500. She said, "No, sir. In fact, we've talked so much about this table that I have been reminded of its true value. As a result, the price is now $1,000."

Unfortunately today far too many single Christians have forgotten their true value, and so they are willing to reduce themselves cheaply in their decisions, thoughts, and actions. What I hope you will do based on the time we have spent together looking at this important subject is to think long, hard, and biblically on your value. When you understand God's view of singlehood and how much He cherishes and treasures you, you will hold your head up high while living single in His arms and care.

One of the most successful singles in Scripture, as I've mentioned, is Joseph. In spite of the fact that he was born into a dysfunctional family, sold into slavery, falsely accused of rape and forgotten in prison—the refrain that we keep hearing about Joseph is that the Lord was with Him and made him a success, even as a single (Genesis 39:2,3, 21, 23).

He had no partner in his life, and yet he was still successful. The key to his success is that phrase: the Lord was with him. But this word "with him" was not in a general sense—omnipresence, after all, God was with everybody. But this phrase lets us know that God was specifically with Joseph in a unique.

The key to your success as a single is this phrase. It is your intimate personal relationship with the Lord, and not just a general religious affiliation.

There must be a greater focus on that relationship than on the circumstances you are in or the marital status you desire to have, but do not have.

So powerful was Joseph's connection with God that he was even able to forgive his brothers who had mistreated him.

The capstone of his life is stated in Genesis chapter 50:19–21 when Joseph said to his brothers that they should not be afraid because their action had taken him to where God wanted him to be. He told them that what they meant it for evil, God turned it around for good in order to bring about this present result to preserve many people alive.

Therefore during your ups and downs—or the roller coaster of your singlehood—make sure that you are practicing God's presence daily. Make sure you are putting intimacy with Jesus Christ as your highest priority so that He can make you successful where you are even in the midst of negative circumstances knowing that He is using them to take you to your destiny. He is taking you to the place He has for you to glorify Him and to advance His kingdom for the benefit of others.

While negative circumstances during your singlehood can seek to push you down and keep you under, your intimacy with Jesus Christ is like a beach ball being forced under water. It is only being set up to be propelled higher. Stick close to Jesus as you wait for Him to unfold the fullness of His plan for you life.

Once you become committed to the principles of this book to wait on, work for and be wedded in the Lord and now that you know your in estimable value as a single, stay married to the Lord (Isaiah 54:5) if or until He changes your status.

http://go.tonyevans.org/singlehood

THE URBAN ALTERNATIVE

The National Ministry of Dr. Tony Evans

Dr. Tony Evans and The Urban Alternative (TUA) **equips, empowers,** and **unites** Christians to **impact** *individuals, families, churches,* and *communities* to restore hope and transform lives.

We believe the core cause of the problems we face in our personal lives, homes, churches, and societies is a spiritual one; therefore, the only way to address them is spiritually. We've tried a political, a social, an economic, and even a religious agenda. It's time for a Kingdom Agenda— God's visible and comprehensive rule over every area of life, because when we function as we were designed, there is a divine power that changes everything. It renews and restores as the life of Christ is made manifest within our own. As we align ourselves under Him, there is an alignment that happens from deep within—where He brings about full restoration. It is an atmosphere that revives and makes whole.

As it impacts us, it impacts others—transforming every sphere of life in which we live. When each biblical sphere of life functions in accordance with God's Word, the outcomes are evangelism, discipleship, and community impact. As we learn how to govern ourselves under God, we then transform the institutions of family, church, and society from a biblically based kingdom perspective where, through Him, we are touching heaven and changing earth.

To achieve our goal we use a variety of strategies, methods, and resources for reaching and equipping as many people as possible.

BROADCAST MEDIA

Hundreds of thousands of individuals experience *The Alternative with Dr. Tony Evans* through the daily radio broadcast playing nearly **1,000 radio outlets** and in over **130 countries**. The broadcast can also be seen on several television networks, and is viewable online at TonyEvans.org.

LEADERSHIP TRAINING

The Kingdom Agenda Pastors (KAP) provides a *viable net-*

work for *like-minded pastors* who embrace the Kingdom Agenda philosophy. Pastors have the opportunity to go deeper with Dr. Tony Evans as they are given greater biblical knowledge, practical applications, and resources to impact individuals, families, churches, and communities. KAP welcomes *senior and associate pastors* of all churches.

The Kingdom Agenda Pastors' Summit develops church leaders to meet the demands of the twenty-first century while maintaining the Gospel message and the strategic position of the church. The Summit introduces *intensive seminars, workshops,* and *resources,* addressing issues affecting the community, family, leadership, organizational health and more.

Pastors' Wives Ministry, founded by Dr. Lois Evans, provides *counsel, encouragement,* and *spiritual resources* for pastors' wives as they serve with their husbands in the ministry. A primary focus of the ministry is the KAP Summit that offers senior pastors' wives a safe place to *reflect, renew,* and *relax* along with training in personal development, spiritual growth, and care for their emotional and physical well-being.

COMMUNITY IMPACT

National Church Adopt-A-School Initiative (NCAASI) prepares churches across the country to impact communities by using *public schools as the primary vehicle for effecting positive social change* in urban youth and families. Leaders of churches, school districts, faith-based organizations, and other nonprofit organizations are equipped with the knowledge and tools to *forge partnerships* and build *strong social service delivery systems.* This training is based on the comprehensive church-based community impact strategy conducted by Oak Cliff Bible Fellowship. It addresses such areas as economic development, education, housing, health revitalization, family renewal, and racial reconciliation. We also assist churches in tailoring the model to meet the specific needs of their communities while simultaneously addressing the spiritual and moral frame of reference.

RESOURCE DEVELOPMENT

We are fostering lifelong learning partnerships with the people we serve by providing a variety of published materials. We offer booklets, Bible studies, books, CDs, and DVDs to strengthen people in their walk with God and ministry to others.

* * *

For more information, a catalog of Dr. Tony Evans' ministry resources, and a complimentary copy of Dr. Evans' devotional newsletter,
call (800) 800-3222
or write TUA at P.O. Box 4000, Dallas TX 75208,
or log on to
www.TonyEvans.org

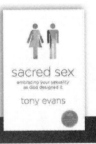

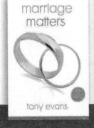

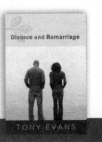

MORE INFORMATION AVAILABLE AT THEKINGDOMAGENDABOOK.COM